Precious Metals Investing On A Budget

Roggie Clark

How to Sell Gold Jewelry for Cash and Avoid Scams

This book was written to help everyday people sell their gold with confidence, protect themselves from common tricks, and get the most money possible.

https://www.amazon.com/Sell-Gold-Jewelry-Avoid-Scams-ebook/dp/B0FW6R6TYN

Learn How To Invest in Gold Bars With This Book

Whether you're new to investing or seeking to diversify your portfolio, this beginner-friendly guide will give you the knowledge and confidence to invest in gold, and other precious metals.

https://www.amazon.com/Ultimate-Investing-Buying-Guide-Beginners-ebook/dp/B0F1KWWDXG

Learn How To Invest in Copper With This Book

Are you ready to take control of your financial future and explore the world of copper investing? Whether you're new to investing or seeking to diversify your portfolio, this beginner-friendly guide will give you the knowledge and confidence to invest in copper.

https://www.amazon.com/Ultimate-Copper-Investing-Buying-Beginners-ebook/dp/B0F892PBSJ

Get Out of Credit Card Debt With This Book

Are you tired of living paycheck to paycheck? Drowning in interest rates and minimum payments that never seem to shrink your balance? *Understanding & Overcoming Credit Card Debt* is your roadmap to financial freedom.

https://www.amazon.com/dp/B0F3WCVWG8

Copyright

Title: Precious Metals Investing On A Budget
Author: Roggie Clark

Disclaimer

The views and opinions expressed in this book are those of the author and do not necessarily reflect the official policy or position of any individual, company, or organization cited or referenced in the text. The author is not affiliated with any of the individuals, companies, or organizations mentioned in the text, nor does the author receive any form of compensation for citing or referencing them.

The professional information in this text is distributed on an "as is" basis, without warranty. While every precaution has been taken in the preparation of the text, neither the author nor the publisher shall have any liability to any person or entity with respect to any loss or damage caused or alleged to be caused directly or indirectly by the instructions contained in this text or by the computer software and hardware products described in it.

The author nor the publisher does not guarantee any specific results or outcomes, and the information provided in this text should not be construed as professional advice. Readers should always consult with a qualified professional before making any significant changes to their website or business.

By reading this text, you agree that the author nor the publisher is responsible for any direct, indirect, incidental, or consequential damages that may arise from the use of the information provided. You assume full responsibility for any actions taken based on the information presented in this text.

Table of Contents

Introduction

Many people are interested in precious metals but never take the first step. The most common reason is not uncertainty about the metals themselves, it is the belief that investing requires more money than they have. When investing is framed around large gold purchases or high dollar strategies, starting small can feel unrealistic or unnecessary.

This book exists to challenge that assumption. Precious metals are not limited to gold and silver alone. They also include platinum and palladium, each with different roles, costs, and market behavior. You do not need large sums of money to begin building exposure to these metals. You need clarity, consistency, and an approach that fits real life finances.

Precious metals serve specific purposes within a broader financial picture. Gold and silver are widely recognized stores of value and tend to be the most accessible for budget focused investors. Platinum and palladium operate differently. They are more closely tied to industrial demand, trade in thinner markets, and often experience sharper price movements. Understanding these differences helps you decide which metals make sense for your situation and which ones can wait.

Throughout this guide, you will learn how gold, silver, platinum, and palladium function as physical assets, how pricing and premiums affect small purchases, and how to build a repeatable strategy with little money. The focus stays practical. You will not be encouraged to chase trends, speculate on short term price swings, or stretch your budget to gain exposure you do not need.

This book is written for everyday investors who want to act deliberately rather than react emotionally. You can read it from start to finish or return to specific chapters as your circumstances change. Either way, the goal remains the same, to help you start responsibly, stay consistent, and move forward with confidence.

By the end of this book, you will understand how to invest in precious metals without overextending your finances. More importantly, you will understand how each metal fits into a budget focused strategy and why starting small, when done thoughtfully, still matters. Let's get started.

Chapter 1: Understanding Precious Metals as Real Assets

Before thinking about prices, strategies, or where to buy, it helps to understand what precious metals actually represent. Gold, silver, platinum, and palladium are not financial products in the traditional sense. They are **physical assets** with intrinsic properties that exist outside of digital systems and paper promises.

This distinction matters, especially when investing on a budget. When you understand why precious metals are different, you are less likely to misuse them or expect them to behave like stocks, savings accounts, or speculative trades.

What Makes Gold, Silver, Platinum, and Palladium Different From Paper Assets

Precious metals do not rely on an issuing authority. They do not depend on earnings reports, management decisions, or debt structures. Their value comes from scarcity, utility, and long term acceptance.

Gold and silver have served as stores of value for thousands of years. Platinum and palladium play a stronger role in industrial applications, which ties their prices more closely to manufacturing demand. Despite these differences, all four metals share one defining trait, they are tangible and finite.

Unlike paper assets, precious metals cannot be created instantly. Supply grows slowly and predictably. This characteristic makes them appealing to investors who want exposure to something real, especially during periods of economic uncertainty.

Why Physical Metals Appeal to Budget Focused Investors

Investing on a budget requires efficiency. Physical precious metals offer a way to convert small amounts of money into assets that are not dependent on financial intermediaries.

Silver often serves as the entry point because of its lower price per ounce. Gold offers stability and liquidity even in small quantities. Platinum and palladium tend to be more expensive and volatile, which makes them less common starting points but still relevant within the broader precious metals category.

For budget focused investors, the appeal lies in ownership rather than scale. Holding a small amount of physical metal still provides diversification and exposure. You do not need large quantities for metals to serve their intended role.

Setting Realistic Expectations From the Start

Precious metals are not designed to generate income or produce rapid gains. They do not pay dividends or interest. Their primary function is preservation, not growth.

Understanding this prevents frustration. When prices move sideways or decline temporarily, informed investors remain patient because they understand the purpose of their holdings. Budget investing benefits from this mindset, as consistency matters more than timing.

Platinum and palladium, in particular, can experience sharp price swings tied to industrial demand. Recognizing this early helps you avoid treating them as short term opportunities rather than long term considerations.

Last Thoughts

Understanding precious metals as real assets sets the foundation for every decision that follows. When you recognize how gold, silver, platinum, and palladium differ from paper based investments, you stop measuring them by the wrong standards.

This chapter establishes perspective rather than strategy. With that perspective in place, you are ready to define what investing on a budget actually means for you. In the next chapter, you will focus on **what investing on a budget really means**, how to set realistic goals, and why consistency matters more than the size of any single purchase.

Chapter 2: What Investing on a Budget Really Means

Investing on a budget is not about limitation. It is about definition. When money is limited, clarity becomes more important than choice. You do not have room for vague goals or impulsive decisions.

This chapter helps you define what investing on a budget truly looks like so your actions align with your reality rather than with someone else's expectations.

Defining Goals When Money Is Limited

Clear goals anchor budget investing. Without them, even small purchases can feel scattered or unproductive. Your goal might be preserving value, diversifying savings, or gradually building tangible assets outside the financial system.

The size of your goal matters less than its direction. A modest, well defined objective creates focus. It also prevents frustration when progress feels slow compared to larger investors.

When you know *why* you are buying precious metals, decisions become easier and mistakes become less likely.

Why Consistency Matters More Than Purchase Size

Budget investing rewards consistency. Small, repeatable purchases over time reduce pressure and smooth out price fluctuations. This approach removes the need to time the market perfectly.

Consistency also builds discipline. Instead of waiting for the perfect moment or saving for a single large purchase, you create a habit. Over time, that habit matters more than the size of any individual transaction.

This principle applies across gold, silver, platinum, and palladium. The right metal matters, but the rhythm of buying matters more.

Avoiding Comparison Traps and Unrealistic Benchmarks

One of the fastest ways to lose confidence is comparing yourself to investors with larger budgets. Their strategies, timelines, and risks do not apply to you.

Budget investing works best when you measure progress against your own plan. Avoid benchmarks that assume unlimited capital or frequent trading. Precious metals investing is not a race.

When you stay focused on your goals and constraints, progress becomes measurable and satisfying, even when it is gradual.

Last Thoughts

Investing on a budget is a strategy, not a compromise. When you define clear goals, commit to consistency, and avoid comparisons that do not serve you, limited money becomes manageable rather than restrictive.

This chapter reframes what progress looks like. With that clarity, you are ready to decide which metals make the most sense when money is limited. In the next chapter, you will compare **gold and silver**, and place **platinum and palladium** in proper context, so you can choose intelligently rather than by default.

Chapter 3: Gold vs Silver vs Platinum vs Palladium – When Money Is Limited

When budgets are tight, choice matters. Gold and silver behave differently, cost different amounts to enter, and respond to market conditions in different ways. Platinum and palladium also exist within the precious metals space, but they do not play the same role for most budget focused investors. Understanding these distinctions helps you avoid default decisions and choose intentionally.

This chapter focuses on access, affordability, and behavior, not predictions.

Cost Differences and Accessibility

Silver is usually the most accessible precious metal. Its lower price per ounce allows you to start with smaller amounts of money and add consistently over time. This makes silver appealing for investors who want flexibility and regular participation.

Gold costs more per ounce, but that higher price often comes with advantages. Gold tends to store value efficiently in smaller physical space and trades in deep, liquid markets worldwide. Even small gold purchases can carry meaningful value and remain easy to sell.

Platinum and palladium typically cost more per ounce and trade in thinner markets. Entry points are higher, and availability can be inconsistent. For budget investors, these metals usually make more sense later rather than at the beginning.

Volatility and Affordability Tradeoffs

Silver prices tend to move more sharply than gold. This volatility can feel uncomfortable, but it also allows gradual buyers to average costs over time. For budget strategies built on consistency, volatility is not automatically a drawback.

Gold usually moves more slowly and predictably. That stability appeals to investors who value preservation over price movement. When money is limited, stability can reduce emotional decision making.

Platinum and palladium often experience sharp price swings tied to industrial demand. These movements can be dramatic, which increases risk for small portfolios. Budget investors benefit from recognizing this volatility rather than chasing it.

Choosing One Metal or Using Both Strategically

Some budget investors focus on one metal to keep things simple. Others use a combination to balance affordability and stability. Both approaches can work.

Silver often provides the foundation because it allows frequent participation. Gold adds balance by concentrating value in smaller amounts. Platinum and palladium usually remain optional, considered only after a core position is established.

The key is alignment. Choose metals that support your goals, budget, and temperament rather than reacting to headlines or short term price moves.

Last Thoughts

Choosing between gold and silver is less about which metal is better and more about which fits your budget and expectations. When money is limited, access, consistency, and behavior matter more than theory.

This chapter helps you place each metal in proper context so you can avoid overextending yourself early. With metal selection clarified, the next step is understanding how pricing actually works. In the next chapter, you will examine **spot price**, **premiums**, and **costs**, and learn how they affect small purchases more than large ones.

Chapter 4: Understanding Spot Price, Premiums, and Costs

Pricing is where many budget investors get discouraged. You see a metal's price quoted online, then discover that buying physical metal costs more than expected. This gap creates confusion and leads some people to believe they are being overcharged. In reality, this difference reflects how physical precious metals are priced and delivered.

Understanding how spot price, premiums, and costs work gives you control. It allows you to evaluate offers accurately and avoid paying more than necessary, especially when investing small amounts.

What Spot Price Actually Represents

Spot price refers to the current market price of a metal in large wholesale markets. It reflects paper contracts and bulk trading, not the cost of producing or delivering physical metal to individual buyers.

Spot price serves as a reference point, not a retail price. It changes constantly and influences all precious metals, including gold, silver, platinum, and palladium. However, it does not account for minting, distribution, or retail overhead.

When you understand spot price as a baseline rather than a promise, pricing conversations become clearer.

Why Premiums Exist and How They Affect Small Buyers

A **premium** is the amount added to the spot price to cover production, handling, shipping, and dealer margins. Physical metal requires real world processes, and premiums reflect those realities.

Premiums tend to affect small buyers more because fixed costs spread across fewer ounces. Buying one ounce usually costs more per ounce than buying larger quantities. This applies across all metals, though silver often carries higher percentage premiums due to manufacturing costs.

Premiums are not inherently bad. They are part of owning physical metal. The key is understanding what is reasonable and avoiding unnecessary markups.

Hidden Costs Beginners Often Overlook

Beyond premiums, other costs can affect your total investment. Shipping fees, payment method charges, and taxes may apply depending on location and seller policies.

Some products also carry embedded costs tied to collectibility or novelty rather than metal content. These extras rarely benefit budget investors and can slow progress without adding value.

Knowing the full cost upfront helps you compare options accurately and choose products that align with your goals.

Last Thoughts

Pricing clarity removes frustration. When you understand spot price, premiums, and additional costs, you stop focusing on individual price gaps and start evaluating value as a whole. This perspective is especially important when investing with limited money.

This chapter equips you to read prices intelligently rather than emotionally. With pricing mechanics clear, the next step is learning how to buy small without overpaying. In the next chapter, you will focus on **low cost entry points**, **small denomination strategies**, and how to avoid products that work against a budget focused plan.

Chapter 5: Buying Small Without Overpaying

When money is limited, every purchase carries more weight. Overpaying early slows progress and creates frustration that can derail consistency. Buying small works best when each decision supports momentum rather than novelty.

This chapter focuses on efficiency. The goal is not to buy everything available, but to buy the *right* things at the *right* time.

Best Low Cost Entry Points

Low cost entry points allow you to participate without stretching your budget. For many investors, this means focusing on widely recognized, easy to resell products rather than specialty items.

Small silver units often serve this role well because they are accessible and familiar to buyers. Modest gold purchases can also make sense when premiums are reasonable and liquidity matters. The key is choosing products that trade easily rather than items that require explanation.

Platinum and palladium usually do not offer low cost entry points. Their higher prices and thinner markets make them better suited for later stages rather than early budget strategies.

Small Denomination Strategies

Small denominations offer flexibility. They allow you to buy consistently, adjust timing, and respond to price changes without committing large sums at once.

However, smaller units often carry higher premiums. The strategy is to balance flexibility with efficiency. Avoid going too small simply for the sake of participation. Choose sizes that keep premiums reasonable while still fitting your budget.

Consistency matters more than precision. A repeatable approach builds confidence and reduces second guessing.

Avoiding Novelty, Hype, and Collector Traps

Budget investors benefit from simplicity. Products marketed for rarity, themes, or collectibility often carry extra costs that do not improve resale value.

Hype driven items may look appealing, but they rarely support long term goals. When money is limited, focus on metal content and market recognition rather than design or promotion.

Ask a simple question before buying, does this product make it easier or harder to sell later. If the answer is unclear, it probably does not belong in a budget focused plan.

Last Thoughts

Buying small works when intention replaces impulse. When you focus on efficiency, recognition, and consistency, limited money becomes a tool rather than an obstacle.

This chapter helps you avoid common pitfalls that slow progress early. With purchasing discipline in place, the next step is choosing where to buy safely. In the next chapter, you will examine **where to buy precious metals**, how to evaluate sellers, and how to compare prices without chasing noise.

Chapter 6: Where to Buy Precious Metals Safely

Choosing where to buy matters just as much as what you buy. For budget investors, mistakes at this stage can be expensive. Overpaying, dealing with unreliable sellers, or misunderstanding terms can undo months of careful planning.

This chapter focuses on safety, transparency, and practicality, not shortcuts.

Online Dealers vs Local Shops

Online dealers offer wide selection and competitive pricing. Their scale often allows lower premiums, especially for common products. Reputable online sellers publish prices clearly and ship directly to you, which simplifies comparison shopping.

Local shops provide immediacy and personal interaction. You can inspect products in person and walk away with metal the same day. However, pricing may vary more widely, and selection can be limited.

Both options can work. Budget investors often benefit from using both, choosing online dealers for efficiency and local shops for flexibility.

What to Look for in a Trustworthy Seller

Trustworthy sellers operate with transparency. They clearly display pricing, explain premiums, and answer questions without pressure. Policies around shipping, returns, and payment methods should be easy to find and easy to understand.

Be cautious of sellers who emphasize urgency, make guarantees, or avoid explaining how prices are calculated. Legitimate sellers expect informed buyers and welcome comparison.

Consistency matters. Sellers who remain in the market through different price cycles tend to be more reliable than those who appear only during high demand periods.

Comparing Prices Without Chasing Noise

Price comparison works best when you focus on total cost, not just advertised premiums. Include shipping, payment fees, and delivery time when evaluating options.

Avoid chasing small differences obsessively. Saving a few dollars matters, but consistency and reliability matter more. Budget investing benefits from repeatable decisions rather than constant switching.

When prices look dramatically better than competitors, pause. Extremely low pricing often comes with tradeoffs that are not immediately visible.

Last Thoughts

Safe buying starts with patience. When you choose transparent sellers, compare total costs, and resist pressure, you protect your budget and your confidence. Where you buy sets the tone for the entire investing experience.

This chapter helps you reduce risk without adding complexity. With safe buying practices established, the next step is avoiding common mistakes that quietly undermine budget strategies. In the next chapter, you will focus on **common budget investor mistakes** and how to steer clear of them early.

Chapter 7: Avoiding Common Budget Investor Mistakes

Mistakes matter more when money is limited. Small missteps can slow progress, reduce confidence, and create unnecessary frustration. The good news is that most budget investor mistakes are predictable and avoidable once you know what to watch for.

This chapter focuses on awareness rather than perfection.

Overtrading and Impulse Buying

Frequent buying and selling may feel productive, but it often increases costs without improving outcomes. Premiums, shipping, and fees add up quickly when transactions pile up.

Impulse buying creates the same problem. Acting on headlines or price spikes leads to scattered holdings and inconsistent progress. Budget investing works best when purchases follow a plan rather than emotion.

Slowing down protects your budget and strengthens discipline.

Chasing Short Term Price Movements

Trying to time short term price moves introduces stress and risk. Precious metals can move unpredictably, especially silver, platinum, and palladium. Budget investors rarely benefit from reacting to these fluctuations.

A consistent approach reduces the need for precision. Instead of chasing dips or spikes, focus on repeatable actions that fit your financial reality.

Price movement becomes noise when your plan is clear.

Buying Too Much Variety Too Early

Variety feels like diversification, but early over diversification often works against budget strategies. Small amounts spread across many products increase premiums and complicate future selling.

Focusing on a narrow set of familiar products improves efficiency and liquidity. Once a foundation is built, adding variety becomes easier and more purposeful.

Clarity beats complexity when resources are limited.

Last Thoughts

Avoiding mistakes does not require perfection. It requires awareness. When you slow down, follow a plan, and resist pressure to react, limited money stretches further and works harder.

This chapter helps you protect progress by recognizing patterns that undermine budget strategies. With mistakes minimized, the next step is securing what you own. In the next chapter, you will explore **storage and security on a budget**, and how to protect physical metals without unnecessary expense.

Chapter 8: Storage and Security on a Budget

Owning physical precious metals means taking responsibility for their safety. This reality can feel intimidating at first, especially when investing on a budget. The good news is that effective storage does not require expensive systems or complicated solutions. It requires thoughtful choices that balance cost, access, and risk.

This chapter focuses on practical protection, not fear driven decisions.

Simple Storage Solutions That Work

For many budget investors, **home storage** is the most practical option. It allows immediate access without ongoing fees and works well for small to moderate holdings.

Simple solutions often work best. Secure locations, discretion, and consistency matter more than complexity. Avoid obvious storage spots and avoid discussing your holdings publicly. Privacy is one of the strongest forms of security.

Small safes, lockable containers, or concealed storage can provide sufficient protection when combined with good judgment.

When Home Storage Makes Sense

Home storage works best when holdings remain within a manageable size and when personal circumstances allow for privacy and control. Budget investors typically fall into this category early on.

As holdings grow, reassessing storage becomes important. This does not mean home storage suddenly fails, but it does mean risk tolerance changes. Security should evolve with value.

Understanding when home storage fits your situation prevents both under protection and unnecessary expense.

Balancing Cost, Access, and Safety

Every storage decision involves tradeoffs. Higher security often reduces access. Greater access can increase exposure. Budget investing requires finding a balance that feels sustainable.

Avoid over spending on storage early. High monthly fees or elaborate systems can quietly undermine progress. Match storage costs to the size and purpose of your holdings.

Security should support your strategy, not compete with it.

Last Thoughts

Storage does not need to be perfect to be effective. When you prioritize discretion, consistency, and proportional security, you protect your metals without draining your budget. Thoughtful storage supports confidence rather than anxiety.

This chapter helps you safeguard what you have built so far. With storage addressed, the next step is understanding how easily precious metals can be sold. In the next chapter, you will explore **liquidity and selling considerations**, and how small holdings move through the market.

Chapter 9: Liquidity and Selling Considerations

Buying precious metals is only half of the equation. Knowing how easily you can sell them, and under what conditions, completes the picture. Liquidity matters more on a budget because flexibility protects you when circumstances change.

This chapter focuses on practicality. The goal is to understand how small holdings move through the market without assuming perfect timing or ideal conditions.

How Easy It Is to Sell Small Holdings

Small, recognizable products tend to sell more easily than obscure or highly specialized items. Familiarity reduces friction. Buyers know what they are looking at and how to price it.

Silver often moves quickly because of affordability and demand. Gold also sells easily due to deep global markets. Platinum and palladium can be liquid, but thinner markets may lead to wider price variation and fewer immediate buyers.

For budget investors, ease of sale often matters more than maximizing every possible dollar.

What Buyers Look for in Budget Sized Positions

Buyers prioritize recognition, condition, and simplicity. Clean, undamaged pieces from well known sources sell more smoothly than unusual formats that require explanation.

Documentation helps. Original packaging, receipts, or basic records can make transactions easier, especially when selling multiple items. While not required, organization signals credibility.

Buyers also consider market conditions. Understanding this context helps you interpret offers realistically rather than personally.

Planning Exits Without Pressure

Selling works best when it is planned rather than forced. Even a loose exit plan provides direction and reduces emotional decisions.

You may sell to rebalance, cover expenses, or take advantage of favorable conditions. Knowing your reasons ahead of time prevents rushed choices. Budget strategies benefit from calm exits rather than reactive ones.

Liquidity supports flexibility. When you understand how and where to sell, you gain confidence without needing to act immediately.

Last Thoughts

Liquidity turns ownership into options. When you understand how easily precious metals can be sold and what buyers expect, you remove uncertainty from the process. This understanding matters most when money is limited and flexibility is valuable.

This chapter prepares you to think about selling before you need to sell. With liquidity clear, the next step is building a strategy that works over time. In the next chapter, you will focus on **building a long term strategy with little money**, and how consistency shapes outcomes more than timing.

Chapter 10: Building a Long Term Strategy With Little Money

A long term strategy matters most when money is limited. Without one, investing becomes reactive and inconsistent. With one, even small amounts of money can compound into meaningful exposure over time.

This chapter focuses on structure. The goal is not perfection, but repeatability.

Creating a Repeatable Buying Plan

A repeatable plan removes guesswork. Decide how often you will buy, how much you are comfortable spending, and which metals fit your goals. Keep the plan simple enough to follow without stress.

Frequency matters more than size. Monthly or quarterly purchases create rhythm and reduce the urge to time the market. When prices fluctuate, your plan continues without emotional interruption.

Write your plan down. Clarity on paper strengthens commitment.

Staying Disciplined During Price Swings

Price movement is unavoidable. Precious metals rise and fall, sometimes sharply. Discipline keeps those movements from dictating behavior.

Avoid changing your plan based on short term price action. Budget investing benefits from steady participation rather than reactive shifts. When prices drop, consistency lowers average cost. When prices rise, restraint prevents overextending your budget.

Discipline protects both money and mindset.

Measuring Progress Realistically

Progress does not always show up in price charts. It shows up in ownership, consistency, and reduced dependence on paper assets.

Measure progress by ounces accumulated, purchases completed, and habits maintained. Avoid benchmarks based on others' portfolios or market hype.

When goals are realistic, progress becomes visible and motivating.

Last Thoughts

A long term strategy transforms limited money into steady action. When you focus on repeatability, discipline, and realistic measurement, investing becomes manageable rather than overwhelming.

This chapter helps you shift from individual purchases to intentional building. With a strategy in place, the final practical considerations come into focus. In the next chapter, you will explore **special situations and life changes**, and how to adapt your approach without abandoning it.

Chapter 11: Special Situations and Life Changes

Budget investing rarely happens in a straight line. Life changes, income fluctuates, and priorities shift. A strategy that works today may need adjustment tomorrow. The key is learning how to adapt without abandoning your approach entirely.

This chapter focuses on flexibility without losing direction.

Windfalls and Unexpected Cash

Occasionally, extra money appears. Tax refunds, bonuses, gifts, or unexpected income can create opportunity, but they can also introduce pressure to act quickly.

When this happens, pause before buying. Decide whether the windfall should strengthen your existing plan or serve a different purpose. Adding to a core position often makes more sense than chasing something new.

Windfalls work best when they reinforce discipline rather than override it.

Pausing, Restarting, or Adjusting Your Strategy

There may be periods when buying is not practical. Expenses rise, income changes, or priorities shift. Pausing does not equal failure. It is part of responsible budgeting.

When circumstances improve, restarting should feel familiar. Return to your original plan, review your goals, and resume at a comfortable pace. Avoid trying to "catch up" by overextending.

Adjustments are normal. Abandonment is optional.

Aligning Metals With Changing Goals

As life changes, so can your reasons for owning precious metals. What began as diversification may shift toward preservation, liquidity, or long term security.

Gold and silver often remain core holdings. Platinum and palladium may become relevant later or may remain unnecessary depending on goals and risk tolerance. Reassessing does not require constant action, only awareness.

Alignment keeps strategy relevant.

Last Thoughts

Special situations test commitment, not knowledge. When you respond thoughtfully to change, you protect both your budget and your progress. Flexibility allows your strategy to grow with you instead of breaking under pressure.

This chapter reinforces the idea that consistency includes knowing when to pause and when to adjust. With life changes addressed, the remaining focus is responsibility. In the next chapter, you will cover **taxes, records, and practical basics**, ensuring your approach remains organized and sustainable over time.

Chapter 12: Taxes, Records, and Practical Basics

As a budget investor, it is easy to focus entirely on buying and forget about the administrative side of investing. While precious metals feel simple because they are physical, basic record keeping and tax awareness still matter. Handling these details properly keeps small investments from becoming unnecessary headaches later.

This chapter focuses on staying organized without adding complexity.

Keeping Simple Purchase Records

You do not need elaborate systems to stay organized. Simple records are enough. Keep receipts, order confirmations, and basic notes for each purchase. Record the date, metal type, quantity, and total cost.

Digital copies work well and reduce clutter. Store everything in one place so information is easy to find when needed. This habit saves time if you decide to sell, rebalance, or answer questions later.

Consistency matters more than detail. Start simple and stay consistent.

General Tax Awareness for Small Investors

Tax rules vary by location and situation, but it is important to understand that selling precious metals may create a taxable event. Profits from sales can be treated as income or capital gains depending on how and when the metals were acquired.

Budget investors often deal with smaller amounts, but that does not remove reporting responsibility. Inherited metals, gifts, and long term holdings may follow different rules. When amounts grow or situations become unclear, consulting a tax professional is a responsible step.

Awareness prevents surprises. Assumptions create problems.

Staying Organized Over Time

Organization supports confidence. When records are current and accessible, decisions feel easier and less stressful. This applies whether you hold metals for years or sell occasionally.

Avoid letting paperwork pile up. Regularly update records after purchases or sales. Small habits prevent large cleanups later.

Practical basics may not feel exciting, but they protect the value of your efforts.

Last Thoughts

Responsible investing includes more than buying wisely. When you maintain simple records and understand basic tax considerations, you protect your time, your money, and your peace of mind. These habits support long term consistency, especially when investing on a budget.

This chapter completes the practical foundation of your strategy. With organization in place, the remaining questions tend to be personal and situational. In the next chapter, you will find **frequently asked questions** that address common concerns and reinforce the guidance throughout this book.

Chapter 13: Frequently Asked Questions

As you build a precious metals strategy on a budget, certain questions tend to surface at the same points in the journey. These questions usually appear when you are deciding whether to start, when you are unsure about a purchase, or when progress feels slow. Addressing them directly helps remove doubt and reinforces confident decision making.

This chapter focuses on clarity, not edge cases.

How Much Is Enough to Start

There is no minimum amount required to begin investing in precious metals. What matters is whether the amount fits your budget without creating stress. Starting small allows you to learn the process, understand pricing, and build habits without pressure.

For many people, the right starting amount is whatever they can invest consistently. Waiting for a larger sum often delays progress unnecessarily. Momentum matters more than size.

Is Silver Better for Beginners Than Gold

Silver often appeals to beginners because of its lower price per ounce and accessibility. It allows frequent participation and flexibility, which fits budget strategies well.

Gold offers stability and strong liquidity, even in small quantities. Some investors prefer to start with silver and add gold later. Others combine both early on. The better choice is the one that aligns with your budget, goals, and comfort level.

Platinum and palladium usually make sense later, once a foundation is established, if they fit your risk tolerance.

What Mistakes Matter Most Early On

The most common early mistakes involve overpaying, chasing short term price moves, and buying too much variety too soon. These actions slow progress and create frustration.

Staying consistent, keeping purchases simple, and following a plan matter more than finding perfect timing or products. Budget investing rewards patience and discipline over complexity.

Last Thoughts

Questions are part of the process, especially when money is limited and decisions feel more personal. When you seek understanding instead of certainty, progress becomes steadier and less stressful.

This chapter reinforces the idea that confidence grows through clarity. With common concerns addressed, you are ready to bring everything together. The final chapter offers closing perspective as you move forward with your precious metals strategy.

Chapter 14: Last Thoughts

Investing in precious metals on a budget is not about finding shortcuts or perfect timing. It is about building a system that works within your reality and staying committed to it over time. When money is limited, clarity and discipline matter more than scale.

Throughout this book, you have learned how gold, silver, platinum, and palladium function as physical assets, how pricing and costs affect small purchases, and how to avoid common mistakes that undermine progress. More importantly, you have learned how to think about investing with intention rather than urgency.

Not every purchase will feel ideal. Prices move, premiums fluctuate, and circumstances change. What matters is consistency. Small, repeatable actions build momentum and confidence, even when progress feels gradual.

Precious metals serve a specific purpose. They preserve value, provide diversification, and offer tangible ownership outside paper systems. You do not need large holdings for them to play that role. You need understanding, patience, and a plan that fits your budget.

If there is one principle to carry forward, it is this, starting small does not mean thinking small. When you invest thoughtfully and stay disciplined, even limited resources can support long term financial resilience.

About the Author

Roggie "Raj" Clark is an entrepreneur and a 10-year marketing professional with a proven track record in e-commerce and digital business growth.

Having built and managed successful online stores with thousands of sales and consulted for numerous marketing clients, Roggie has mastered the intricacies of online marketing, branding, and consumer behavior. He has also written several popular books on digital marketing, SEO (search engine optimization), and programming (HTML, CSS, and JavaScript).

As a former marketing manager at a fintech company—a role he secured through his own marketing and financial expertise—Roggie gained firsthand experience in financial strategy and wealth-building.

This journey inspired him to share insights with amateur investors, helping them save money, make smarter financial decisions, and build long-term wealth. Raj currently lives in Maryland with his sister and niece.

www.ingramcontent.com/pod-product-compliance
Lightning Source LLC
LaVergne TN
LVHW022322200926
848481LV00004B/1400
* 9 7 9 8 2 9 5 5 4 5 1 0 8 *